THE STUPID TERM PAPER:
How to Plan It, Write It, and Get an "A" on It

Published by G8 Press
P.O. Box 9043
Cedarpines Park, CA 92322-9043
www.G8press.com

TABLE OF CONTENTS

❧

INTRODUCTION

So you have to write a stupid term paper. You're probably thinking something like:

- ➢ This is impossible.
- ➢ I can't do this.
- ➢ My life is already complicated enough without this pressure.
- ➢ This is going to be hard.
- ➢ My social life is going to be ruined because of this junk.
- ➢ I'll find some way to get out of this.
- ➢ What a waste of time; I'll never use this skill in "real life".

I'm feelin' you. At first glance, this assignment does seem like it's going to be way too much to handle, hard and time-consuming. You've worked hard on getting a social life right where you want it, and now here comes something to cut into valuable free time. Or perhaps you're working a job and going to school, so the hours spent at work is a hindrance to getting this paper written. And after school, you can't see how writing papers is going to be a skill that will make any money, so why, why, why go through all this stress?

Well, technically, you do have a choice. Refuse to write the paper. Of course, you'll fail the class, have to retake it, and possibly won't graduate. You'll be the life of all your friends' college going-away parties and help them pack up their stuff, load it into their cars, and wave goodbye as they jubilantly ride off into promising futures – without you.

You'll leave that last party and change into your paper hat or apron or lame beige and orange striped uniform shirt with khaki pants, to be off to your minimum-wage-paying job. All because you refused to write the stupid term paper.

When your parents get the news that you won't be graduating, they'll flip. After all, they were looking forward to your exit from their house and entrance to a university in about six-to-nine months. They had planned to remodel your room into an audio-visual center with a large-screen TV, mood lighting, and a non-alcoholic mini-bar. Now they turn into unrecognizable people when a two-month deadline is given to get an apartment and pay for your own trifling lifestyle. But you didn't write the stupid term paper. At least you stuck to your principles. After all, that's the important thing, right?

This scenario isn't that far from the truth if you decide to blow off this term paper assignment. You don't want to be the one who doesn't graduate, who's left behind when friends go off to college, who's supporting himself at a dead-end job and not living large like you planned.

So, since this term paper is standing between you and a glorious future, it's time to knock this thing out. This book will help write one of the most dazzling term papers a teacher has ever seen. Not only that, you'll be able to use this model to impress college professors at both the undergraduate and graduate levels. Ready? Let's do this!

WHAT THE HECK IS A TERM PAPER, ANYWAY?

What the heck is a term paper, anyway? Good question. A term paper is basically a research assignment. It actually could also be called a research paper except it's longer and it goes farther than reports you wrote in elementary, middle, and early high school. In those reports, you basically looked information up in encyclopedias, books, websites, and other sources, and "reported" on what was read, probably five-to-ten pages.

A large part of a term paper requires the same thing in fifteen-to-twenty pages. However, in a term paper, you have to have something to say *about* the topic, not just report *on* the topic, and make some sort of educated comment. Look at the examples below and see the difference:

A Report Says...	A Term Paper Says...
America has participated in many wars.	America has participated in many wars and uses war for economic gain.
Slavery was devastating to African-Americans.	The mentality thrust upon African-Americans during slavery still exists and hinders the advancement of Black people today.
The death penalty has been a part of many cultures throughout history.	Even though the death penalty has been a part of many cultures throughout history, the flawed legal system in the United States makes it impossible to administer fairly, so it should be abolished.

Got the idea? Your term paper will be about a topic on which you have something to say, a position on which you want to take a stand, a point to prove, and faults to expose.

Okay, so now let's get the timetable together.

2

ESTABLISH A TIMETABLE

In his work entitled *Night Thoughts*, author Edward Young said, "Procrastination is the thief of time." You may have heard this quote when sitting around watching T.V. or listening to music instead of doing homework or taking care of chores. Isn't it funny how you can always find something else to do besides the work for which a grade will be received?

When a project must be completed, but you keep putting it off, it's called procrastination. As the saying above shows, procrastinating literally steals time, because once time is gone, that's it. You can't get it back.

With this in mind, it is extremely important that you establish and then stick to a timetable – a schedule that will monitor progress as you research and write this term paper. Here's how to establish a timetable:

STEP ONE: Know the due date.

Find out when the paper is due. Determine to finish your paper at least one week before that final date. On a big project like this, it's always a good idea to factor in time for the unexpected. Anything could happen during the course of several months. There could be problems finding resources, computers crash or freeze – lots of crazy things, even sickness, can happen. Remember Murphy's Law, "Anything that can go wrong, will go wrong."

STEP TWO: Count the days.

Start with today, count the number of days there are between now and the due date for the term paper. The number of days you have between today and the day before the due date is your work window. In other words, this is how long you have to do all the stuff required to complete an "A" paper.

At the beginning of the quarter or semester, you will know if a term paper is due in that class. Read the class syllabus carefully. In addition to other information like necessary textbooks and test dates, this syllabus should give the due date for the paper. Count the days, as soon as you know that a paper will be due, and start work immediately.

STEP THREE: Plan your attack.

The topics covered in chapters 3 – 14 will help plot out an attack plan for writing your term paper. Look at how many days you have and match that with how much is to be done. This will give an idea of how long you can reasonably spend on each item.

For example, if given three months to complete the paper, that's about 91 days or about 13 weeks. If you don't want to do any work on Saturdays and Sundays, that reduces the work window to 65 days. Figure in five emergency/Murphy's Law days and it's down to 60 days total. Plot your plan as follows:

Item to Complete	Week #	# of Days	Actual Calendar Dates
Find a topic	1	5	Sept. 1-5
Do preliminary research	2	5	Sept. 8-12
Write thesis statement	3	2	Sept. 15-16
Formulate outline	3	3	Sept. 17-19
Do more research	4-6	15	Sept. 22-Oct. 10
Compose introduction	7	3	Oct. 13-15
Write preliminary conclusion	7	2	Oct. 16-17
Write sections (w/ endnotes)	8-10	14	Oct. 20-Nov. 6
Write final conclusion	10	1	Nov. 7
Format bibliography	11	3	Nov. 10-12
Check format	11	2	Nov. 13-14
Pull it together (final touches)	12	5	Nov. 17-21

In the above scenario, you will complete the paper in 60 days, without working on the weekend, and the paper can be turned in five days early.

Of course, this is in the perfect world – the world in which none of us live. When figuring a timetable, plan for other activities that crowd into life. In addition to the work which has to be completed for other classes, be sure to include extra-curricular activities; sports practice and games, club meetings and functions, and volunteer hours to complete. You may attend church and have weekly or monthly obligations there. Special days, like a birthday or holidays, may fall within this time frame when you won't want to work on it. Many students hold part-time jobs that swallow up considerable chunks of time. And let's not forget a social life. All these considerations must be taken into account when scheduling the work time spent on this very important term paper assignment.

What am I saying? I'm preparing you for reality. If the goal is to get a great grade on this term paper, as the saying goes, you'd better recognize! Time will be crunched and you'll have to be one incredibly organized individual, juggling balls and keep plates spinning. A precisely planned and strictly-followed schedule – a firm timetable – is the only way you're going to finish successfully. Otherwise, blood pressure may rise to dangerous levels, friends could be lost, and because of stress, expletives were spoken.

Now pull out a calendar and use the table on the next page to establish a personal timetable for completing your paper.

Timetable Plan

Today's date: _____ Term paper due date: _____

# of weeks to work: _____ # of days to work: _____

Item to Complete	Week #	# of Days	Actual Calendar Dates
Find a topic			
Do preliminary research			
Write thesis statement			
Formulate outline			
Do more research			
Compose introduction			
Write preliminary conclusion			
Write sections (w/ endnotes)			
Write final conclusion			
Format bibliography			
Check format			
Pull it together (final touches)			

Planned completion date: _____

Now, let's move on to find a suitable topic.

3

FIND YOUR TOPIC

The first step in writing a great term paper is finding a great topic. There are several things to think about before choosing a topic. You will have to:

> ➢ deal with this topic for several months, and
> ➢ read a lot of different stuff about this topic.

You will also have to:

> ➢ find lots of different stuff about this topic,
> ➢ understand what you read about this topic, and
> ➢ explain what you have read about this topic.

With these points in mind, ***choose a topic that interests you***. You will not do a good job if a topic is boring because lots of reading on the subject is required. The mind will not think of questions about a topic in which you have no interest.

"But, suppose my teacher or professor assigns me a topic I don't like?" (You're not going to like this answer.) That's the breaks. It is still required to complete the project and it is incumbent upon you to do the best work because you need the "A". However, even if given something specific to write on, find your own slant. So, if you are required to do a term paper about slavery, slant it toward the lasting effects slavery has had on the broken African-American family in current society. If you are required to write a term paper on World War II, slant it to discuss how the personalities of the major leaders affected the outcome of the war. Get the idea?

In college, the subjects of papers will have to have something to do with the course you're taking. For example, in an introduction to psychology class, you could be required to write a term paper on any subject that's covered in the textbook. In an environmental science class I took in college, I had to do just that. One of the last chapters of our text covered pollution. Now that's something I had experienced because I was a native of Los Angeles, California, and I was used to smog. My term paper explained the smog problem in Los Angeles and suggested a possible solution.

Fortunately, the topic of a high school term paper is usually your choice within certain parameters. You will probably be allowed to choose any topic out of anything possible in the universe, as long as the teacher approves. That approval will be based upon appropriateness of the topic and the teacher's evaluation as to whether or not you will be able to cover it adequately in the amount of pages or words required.

Appropriate

Once, one of my students wanted to write a term paper about pornography. I trusted that this student would handle the topic in an honest, mature manner. He did neither. Not only did his research ignore the negative aspects of porn, he sprinkled pictures and lewd remarks throughout the project. His treatment of the subject was indeed inappropriate. All he really wanted was an excuse to surf indecent internet sites.

There are plenty of topics to choose from that will not require exposure to lewd information. If attending a religious school, teachers may give caution when writing term papers about the occult or the supernatural. Religious people understand the reality of the spirit world and realize young people are vulnerable to its influences. Again, there are innumerable other topics to choose that will be both fascinating and safe.

Also consider whether or not your parents approve of the chosen topic for your term paper. After all, this information will get into your head. If parents have strong opinions on this thesis, your knowledge may cause friction at home. Perhaps it would be better to save controversial topics until you're out of the house, in college and living on your own. And think about this, since the later high school years are times when parents are feeling pretty left out, involving them in this term paper is a great way to include them in your life.

Who knows? Having your parents work with you on the paper may have several positive effects. First, they will be so interested that they will actually help with research and ideas, thus cutting work down a little. Second, they will see how dedicated you are to school work. This is sure to raise their pride level. Finally, because you are so dedicated, you will be seen as responsible and may be given a little more freedom in other areas.

Adequate

Topics cannot be too narrow or too broad. A topic that is too narrow (Volkswagen Spark Plugs) can be thoroughly discussed in two pages. A topic that is too broad (World Leaders: Past and Present) will take volumes of books to cover completely; the twenty-page maximum won't even begin to scratch the surface on all that has to be said. When deciding upon a topic, be sure there is enough information found to talk intelligently for 15 – 20 pages.

Topics must be scholarly. Don't choose something that has little or no academic relevance. Forget about doing papers on hula hoops, earrings, picture frames, or noses. Go instead for ideas dealing with historical events, amazing discoveries, interesting people and places, or socially relevant issues.

Got Ideas?

Write them here!

IDEA WORKSHEET

To help select a topic that will be a perfect fit, use the following prompts to brainstorm. Write what comes to mind under each column. These ideas will then be the raw material that will spark a winning idea.

Stuff that interests me	Things that make me mad
Things I've wondered about. (*I wonder why...?*)	Something should be done about...
What's the big deal about...?	_____ is better than that _____
This should be illegal	This should be legal
This should be abolished	This should be started
This should be changed	_____ is the cause of _____
The solution for _____ is _____	What's the difference between _____ and _____?

SAMPLE

Stuff that interests me	Things that make me mad
Things I've wondered about. (*I wonder why...?*)	Something should be done about...
What's the big deal about...?	_____ is better than that _____
This should be illegal	This should be legal
This should be abolished	This should be started
This should be changed	_____ is the cause of _____
The solution for _____ is _____	What's the difference between _____ and _____?

Now read over the ideas you've written on the idea worksheet. Highlight or circle four or five ideas that seem really good. Make sure these four or five fit the criterion:

- ➢ The topic interests you
- ➢ The topic is appropriate
- ➢ The topic is adequate
  - o Not too narrow
  - o Not too broad
  - o Scholarly

Toss out any topic that does not pass the criterion test. Then, take the remaining topics to your instructor for approval. Once the possible topics are approved, you are ready to do preliminary research.

DO PRELIMINARY RESEARCH

You've decided upon four or five possible topics, but is the information needed readily available? Check four places to find out how much is written about each of your possible topics. Use the chart that starts on page 17 to keep track of this preliminary research.

#1 – The Internet

Surf the net to see what sites are available concerning your topic. Don't just look at the list of topics that comes up though. Many entries are duplicates, so you might think there are more sites than there really are. Open some of the sites and scan what's there. Look for sites that contain a variety of information, are written by different authors of various backgrounds, and sponsored by different organizations.

When you find great sites, be sure to bookmark the website addresses to get back to them when in-depth research begins.

#2 – Books

Next, go to the library and search for books written about each of your possible topics. Again, check for a variety of authors from different backgrounds.

For example, use books written by people who have college degrees in the subject as well as books written by people with practical, everyday experience with the topic. Look for the most current information by checking the copyright date. However, don't disregard old books. It will be interesting to discover how thought on your topic has changed, grown, and been revised over the years.

#3 – Magazines

While in the library, the next type of resource to check is periodicals. Magazines are called periodicals because they are published periodically, usually monthly, bimonthly (every other month), or quarterly (4 times a year). This means the information in magazine articles is much more up-to-date than the information found in books.

The Guide to Periodical Literature can be found either in booklet form or on the library's computers. Simply look up or type in the topic of interest to find the list of publications that have recently published articles about that topic. The entry will tell you the name of the magazine, the date of the issue, the title of the article, the name of the author, the page number of the article, and whether or not there are pictures.

Make a list of the articles you might want to use. Go to the stacks to look at the articles or keep the list to go back and read the articles later. Remember, this is only preliminary research, to find out if there is enough information on your subject to adequately cover the topic in a 15-20 page paper.

#4 – Media Resources

The library and T.V. Guide can help with this one. Movies, documentaries, and programs on the History Channel and the Discovery Channel are also fair game and great places from which to gather information. That's right, you read it correctly. Some research can be done watching television. Find out what videos exist that discuss your subject. Place them on reserve with the librarian to be sure to get them when needed. Use the T.V. Guide to find out what's going to be shown on the History and Discovery Channels. The internet can probably be used to find out what programs have been shown in the past and how you can obtain a copy of the video or DVD to watch at home.

As you look over the internet sites, books, or magazines, scan the information to get a sense of how authors approached the topic. Make a few notes regarding how to plan and approach it. Perhaps, when looking through sources, it becomes obvious that a particular slant has no or very little consideration. Maybe more questions than answers jump to mind. That's a good thing. You have hit upon a slant that research can further explore.

Also, deliberately search for sources that present opposing points of view so that your term paper presents a balanced, honest discussion of as many sides as possible. The conclusion you draw or the point you prove will be more scholarly if compared to a wide variety of sources and if you present an in-depth, honest look at all sides of the issue or topic.

Once information is gathered on all four or five of the prospective topics (use pages 17-18 for assistance here), look over the chart and choose the one topic that has lots of information and interests you the most. Congratulations! You have chosen your term paper topic!

Write your chose term paper topic here: _____

Preliminary Research Tracking Chart

Possible Topic #1: _____

Internet Sites	Books
Magazine Articles	Media Resources

My Planned Approach: _____

Possible Topic #2: _____

Internet Sites	Books
Magazine Articles	Media Resources

My Planned Approach: _____

Possible Topic #3: _____

Internet Sites	Books
Magazine Articles	**Media Resources**

My Planned Approach: _____

Possible Topic #4: _____

Internet Sites	Books
Magazine Articles	**Media Resources**

My Planned Approach: _____

5

FORMULATE YOUR THESIS STATEMENT

Your thesis statement is the quarterback of the term paper. Whatever play the quarterback calls, the team performs. In the same way, whatever the thesis statement says is what your paper will do. So, if the thesis statement claims your paper will compare the human brain to the computer and prove that no machine will ever supersede the powers of the brain, then that's what the paper must discuss – no more, no less.

The thesis statement defines your approach. Use the following list to check which approach is most suitable for the manner in which you are thinking of dealing with your topic.

Possible Approaches:

_____ Analysis   Break your topic into small pieces, explaining each piece to prove your point.

_____ Causes   Explain what has caused or what causes something to happen and prove what has to be done to stop the causes (if they are negative), or help the causes (if they are positive).

_____ Chronology   Discuss the development of a movement and prove why that development is important or how it has affected something (people, society, etc.)

_____ Comparison   Compare two things, proving how one is better than the other, and showing why this is significant to society.

_____ Con   Speak out against something proving its detriment and suggesting how to fix it.

_____ Differences   Discuss how things within a category differ and comment upon the significance of these differences.

_____ Effects   Explain the effects of something and prove the outcome. Then suggest how to reverse negative effects.

_____ Literary Themes   Discuss something about literature proving its impact.

_____ Pro   Speak out in favor of something proving its benefit and suggest ways to implement, make more acceptable, etc.

_____ Problem   Expose a problem, prove why it's a problem, and suggest solutions.

_____ Solutions   Pose a solution to a problem and prove why this is the best solution by comparing it with other solutions that have failed.

I bet you could use an example before you try to write your own thesis statement, right? Okay, look back at page 11, the sample idea worksheet. The fifth box down on the left. Suppose you were really concerned about the welfare system in the United States. Let's say you believe the system has lots of problems and should be abolished. Take the *topic* of the welfare system, and use it as the subject of your thesis statement. Then state your *opinion* and your *position* in the predicate of the thesis statement.

Now look back at the possible approaches listed on pages 19 and 20. For this welfare system topic, you would have checked "Problem" on page 20. Your thesis statement would be outlined like this:

Subject: the welfare system
Opinion: problematic
Approach: problem
Position: (what my paper intends to prove): should be abolished

Then the thesis statement would be structured like this:

The welfare system   is so problematic that it should be abolished.
    SUBJECT   PREDICATE

See? It's simple. Now go back to the Preliminary Research Tracking Chart from chapter four. Choose a topic. Settle on your approach from the list in this chapter. Now put that all together by writing one sentence that identifies your topic and states the approach, making it clear what the term paper intends to prove.

Use this page to draft and revise your thesis statement. Write a finalized thesis statement at the bottom of this page.

Finalized Thesis Statement: _____

_____

_____

6

ARRANGE YOUR OUTLINE

It is now time to draft the outline for your term paper. Since time has been spent in preliminary research, you have some ideas of what to talk about. If the thesis statement is your quarterback, the outline is your playbook. Each "play" will be a section, and each section will take you the length of the "field" from introduction to conclusion. Just as you wouldn't use any plays that will keep you from reaching your goal, unrelated information to your subject in your paper would not lead toward the conclusion.

Another way to look at the outline is to see it as a map. Certain roads taken will get you from home to a destination. "Home" is your thesis statement. Your "destination" is the conclusion. The sections of the paper will be the roads you take to get from home to your destination. Be sure all of the sections (roads) lead to your destination (conclusion), and be sure one section (road) leads smoothly into the next section (road). Don't take any side trips. Don't wander from the main path.

So, what needs to be said? What information is necessary to get the audience to understand what your topic is all about? What background information relates directly to your topic? What questions have to be answered in order to reach the conclusion you want to prove? What arguments must be discounted in order for the point to be proven?

Start by looking back at the approach chosen in chapter five. What does the description of your approach say? Here is the first clue as to what must be included in the outline. Let's use our welfare system example. The description of the problem approach says, "You will expose a problem, prove why it's a problem, and suggest solutions." Looks like a great start for an outline. The starting outline for this paper would look like this:

Thesis statement:	The welfare system is so problematic that it should be abolished.

    I.   Exposing the Problems of the Welfare System

    II.   Proving how the Problems are Negatively Effecting Society

    III.   Solutions to the Problems of the Welfare System

Of course, this is only the first skeleton of the full outline. Every paper needs a great introduction (we'll discuss that in chapter 8) and a conclusion. Also, most papers need some kind of discussion of the background of the subject itself. So now the outline will grow to look like this:

Thesis statement:	The welfare system is so problematic that it should be abolished.

    I.   Introduction
    II.   Background of the welfare system in the United States
    III.   Exposing the Problems of the Welfare System
    IV.   Proving how the Problems are Negatively Effecting Society
    V.   Solutions to the Problems of the Welfare System
    VI.   Conclusion

Now it's simply a matter of filling in the sub-points that will explain each section. The sub-points should answer as many of the five basic questions about that section – who, what, when, where, why, and how – as possible. The sub-points may also be a list of things that explains the section. Later, you may need to add smaller points under some of your sub-points. These will be numbered numerically.

Perhaps this outline will end up looking something like this:

Thesis statement: The welfare system is so problematic that it should be
                      abolished.

I.   Introduction

II.   Background of the welfare system in the United States

    A. When the system began

    B. Who started the system

    C. Why the system was begun

    D. The original intent of how the system was supposed to work

III.   Exposing the Problems of the Welfare System

    A. Problem #1

    B. Problem #2

    C. Problem #3

    D. Problem #4

IV.   Proving how the Problems are Negatively Effecting Society

    A. How Problem #1 is Negatively Effecting Society

    B. How Problem #2 is Negatively Effecting Society

    C. How Problem #3 is Negatively Effecting Society

    D. How Problem #4 is Negatively Effecting Society

V.   Solutions to the Problems of the Welfare System

    A. Replace how the System is handling Problem #1 with _____

    B. Replace how the System is handling Problem #2 with _____

    C. Replace how the System is handling Problem #3 with _____

    D. Replace how the System is handling Problem #4 with _____

VI.   Conclusion

Now it's your turn. Use the bottom of this page to write down a starting outline. Then, turn to the next page and use the outline template as a jumping off point. Write the thesis statement at the top of the outline template. Start with the approach selected in chapter five. Use the description of that approach and formulate a starting outline. Now add the introduction section at the beginning and the conclusion section at the end. If your paper lends itself to the need for historical background, add that between the introduction and section one. Now refine the sections needed that you chose from the approach description. Add any other sections needed to fully explain your topic. Now add the sub-points.

IMPORTANT NOTE:

Sometimes the grade received on a term paper will determine your grade in the class, so once you start typing, protect the work. Save work in three places: on the hard drive, on a flash drive, and as a hard copy. Every day you work on the project, save it, back it up on the flash drive, and print out the new pages. All of this is just a precaution against power surges, power outages, and unintentional deletions. Hopefully, you'll never need these back-ups, but if you do, they are far more comforting than receiving flowers at the hospital while recovering from the heart attack brought on if data is lost.

Outline Template

Thesis Statement: _____

I.   Introduction

II.   Background of _____

    A. Sub-point 1

    B. Sub-point 2

    C. Sub-point 3

III. Section One

    A. Sub-point 1

    B. Sub-point 2

    C. Sub-point 3

IV.   Section Two

    A. Sub-point 1

    B. Sub-point 2

    C. Sub-point 3

V.   Section Three

    A. Sub-point 1

    B. Sub-point 2

    C. Sub-point 3

VI.   Conclusion

If you scribbled notes beside the outline on the previous page, it's time to cut the apron strings. Go to the computer and type out your full outline. Don't panic. You can do this. Keep page 26 beside you as you type. Don't be afraid; now's the time to venture out and make this your own. You may have five rather than three major sections and sub-points that go from "A" through "E". There may be obvious smaller points that you will list numerically under sub-points.

Whatever you have to add to make the outline clear, do it. Remember, this is the map that will move you efficiently and effectively from your thesis statement to your conclusion. Spend time making clear what each section will include. This will not only help the instructor know your purpose, it will keep you on track while putting the paper together. When finished typing up your outline, take a copy to your instructor for comments and approval.

The typed outline will be included when you turn in the term paper. It will serve as a detailed table of contents without page numbers. Follow the format guidelines on page 51 for the proper way to indent your outline.

Type your outline in a separate file from the text of your paper because the outline is not a part of your 15 – 20 page count. However, you must use lower case Roman numerals as the page numbers on your outline. The style of page number can be found as you go through the pull-down menus in the computer's page number format area.

7

DO MORE RESEARCH AND BUILD YOUR BIBLIOGRAPHY

Now that your outline is drafted, writing the rest of your term paper will be a breeze. Start with the section following your introduction. (We'll get back to the introduction later.) Read all the information in your researched print sources that pertains to this section. Make notes to yourself. Watch the videos, movies, and documentaries you have identified. Interview people. Again, write down notes.

You will continue to bounce back and forth from research to writing for the rest of this process. Be careful to stick to the timetable you decided upon way back in chapter two. Also, be sure to keep a detailed list of all the resources you are using. You will need this information for you bibliography and your endnotes.

Your Bibliography

As you wade through the stacks of printed material that should now be gathering all over your bedroom, it will be easy to lose track of what you've read. I don't want that to happen to you. It is required that you supply a comprehensive list of all the sources you used in your research. This list will be located at the end of your term paper and will be entitled "Works Cited" which is simply another name for the bibliography.

A 15 – 20 page term paper requires that you use approximately 15 – 30 resources or more. And it's imperative that you use at least three (if not more) **_different types_** of sources. I mean, all your sources cannot come from the internet. You shouldn't use all books, all magazines, or all documentaries. Get some of your information from the internet, some from books, some from magazine articles, some from encyclopedias, etc. Mix it up.

I know what you're thinking. _That's a lot of reading!_ Well, you're right. You want to get a great grade on this paper, don't you? Of course you do. This is what it will take.

You may ask, "Why do I have to start making this list of sources so early? Can't I just wait until I've finished writing the paper and then stack all the resources up and write down the names of all the titles?"

Nice try, Sherlock, but no cigar. If you still haven't caught on, this term paper project is a long one. You will not craft this puppy overnight – not even in two or three nights. Books that you used for the research of section two, may have to be returned to the library before you even think about writing section five. Also, some resources will be surprises to you. You may hear a quote on the radio or see a billboard that directly relates to your subject. If you don't jot that down at the time, the particulars about the source could be lost to you forever. There's no book to go back to in these cases.

So, use the following page as your central location for keeping track of your sources. For each resource, write down the following information:

- Title (of the book, magazine, encyclopedia, website, movie, TV show, documentary, name of person interviewed, etc.)
- Author
- Name of article (Make a note of page numbers for quotes used. Page numbers will be necessary for endnotes, not for the bibliography.)
- Publisher
- Publisher's city
- Publication/Copyright date

Okay, so keep doing your research. Go section by section through your outline, reading and jotting down notes. It's now time to move into the writing phase.

Keep Track of Resources:

8

COMPOSE YOUR INTRODUCTION

You are totally immersed in the writing of the term paper by now. A fair amount of research about your topic has been done, so now you should be able to come up with a dynamite way to start the paper.

Think about the first time you see a really good-looking person of the opposite sex. The hair, the clothes, the shoes, the curves or the muscles, the smile, the twinkle in the eyes – everything is perfect! You can't stop looking. In fact, you go out of the way to keep looking and start formulating a plan to get to know that person better. All of this is because of the first impression that person's appearance made.

Writing the introduction is your term paper's first impression and it serves several purposes:

- Piques your audience's interest in the topic – catches your audience's attention
- Lets the audience know what your paper will be about
- Sets the tone of the paper by revealing your position and approach
- Provides a road map that reveals how you plan to move to the conclusion

The term paper introduction has at least three parts – the opening, your thesis statement, and elements of the outline. A transition between your opening and the thesis statement might be needed to make the introduction flow smoothly.

<u>Openings</u>

#1 – Use a Quote

At the beginning of Chapter 2, a quote was used to catch your attention. The chapter was about establishing a timetable and the old saying, "Procrastination is the thief of time" summed up in a few words a principle that is important to grasp.

Since communication of ideas is central to the educational process, it's important to be able to get your thoughts across to others in an easily-understood manner. The ability to communicate ideas effectively is what makes an author great. We are able to read their work and use some of their phrases to make our own points clear when we are trying to communicate with others.

So with this in mind, have you heard any thought-provoking quotes made by authors, statesmen, religions leaders, or even musicians that might fit the subject of your term paper?

For example, if writing a paper about fear, you might work F.D.R's famous quote into the introduction: "The only thing we have to fear is fear itself." If your paper is trying to convince people of their duty to military service for their country, you might quote Nathan Hale who said, "I only regret that I have but one life to lose for my country." And if blasting racial profiling, Dr. Martin Luther King, Jr.'s quote can be used when he declared that he wished his children could "live in a nation where they will not be judged by the color of their skin, but by the content of their character." Appropriate verses of Scripture from the Bible make great quotes to use as well. You get the idea.

Of course, you have to work the quote into the introduction. Don't just toss in a quote and move to the next section of the paper. Explain why you are using this particular quote. Let the audience know what this quote has to do with the point your paper is going to try to make. Also, always attribute the quote. Let the audience know who said it.

Suppose you don't know any great quotes. No problem. There are available sources. My favorite is a really thin book entitled *Familiar Quotations* by John Bartlett (Little, Brown & Company). When looking up key words in the index, you'll find a whole list of times that word was used by famous or important people. The word will be listed in a partial phrase. Read down the list until there's a phrase that fits your needs. Then flip to the page indicated and read the whole quote. There you will also find out who said it and where it was published.

There are websites with tons of quotes. Here are a few approved sites:

www.columbia.edu/acis/bartleby/bartlett

www.cybernation.com/victory/quotations/directory.html

www.quotablequotes.net

www.quoteland.com

#2 – Ask a Question

A question introduction is about the easiest one to use to catch the reader's attention. Simply pose several questions that your paper will answer.

For example, a paper exposing the evils of the welfare system, begins by asking, "Did you know that the United States government pays perfectly healthy people not to work? Or that the government pays some women for having babies – the more babies they have, the more money they get?" Therefore, in the introduction state, "These and other unbelievable facts are just the tip of the iceberg when discussing how out of control the welfare system in America has become."

As seen from the above example, pose your question in such a way as to shock the audience and then in your paper explain the allegations made.

#3 – Make a Comment

The comment introduction basically states why you became interested in the topic of your term paper. Somewhat like the question introduction, the comments must be worded so they move the audience to be interested too.

Sometimes statistics can be shocking. Perhaps you hear that a large percentage of university freshmen drop out of their first year of college. This is worrisome. Why does this happen and is there a chance of it happening to you? The introductory comments could be worded as follows:

> Recently the U. S. News and World Report stated that 75% of university freshmen from the inner city drop out of college during the first year. They just can't cut it. As a high school senior, looking forward to my first year of college, this statistic scares me. I am wondering if I'm ready or not. I wanted to find out what was causing this high drop-out rate so I could put together a plan to avoid those causes. College freshmen can put together a strategy that will enable them to avoid becoming part of the drop-out statistic.

#4 – Tell a Story

The story introduction is the longest one you'll write. In it, retell an incident or anecdote that relates directly to the point of your thesis. Here are some examples of topics for which a story might fit as a good lead:

Topic	Story Lead
Keeping marijuana illegal	Tell about how a person's life was ruined because of marijuana use.
Racial profiling	Relate the experience of a Black executive being stopped by the police for no apparent reason other than driving a nice car in a predominately White neighborhood.
Topic	Story Lead
Evils of the welfare system	Recount how 3 generations of one family have not broken out of the government-assistance cycle.

It would be great if your story is an actual personal experience of your own. You will be able to relate the story with feeling so that your audience can catch your emotions. However, feel free to retell someone else's story, as long as you tell it using visuals and lots of detail. Choose to use the story introduction only if that story has really touched you in a special way. It would be even better if you could find a story to which you can point throughout your paper. So, in addition to introducing your paper with part of the story, you would use other parts of the same story as examples of points you are making throughout your paper. And always remember to retell stories in the past tense.

For example, if you were writing about the marijuana topic above, in your introduction, you would relate the general story about Johnnie and how he had a promising future until he started using marijuana. Then, in the section of your paper about marijuana's negative effects on the human body, you would discuss the facts and then tell how Johnnie experienced these effects. In the section of your paper about how marijuana is addictive, you would show Johnnie's addictive behaviors. In other words, you could continue to weave Johnnie's story through your entire paper.

Find stories that match your thesis in a variety of places:
- Your own personal experiences
- Your family's or friends' personal experiences
- The source material you are reading on your topic
- Television news
- Documentaries
- A person you are interviewing in connection with research on your topic

You may be surprised to find that many people are quite willing to talk to you about even the most sensitive subjects. It may be necessary to change the names of people who are still living in order to be sensitive to their need for anonymity or privacy, but that's acceptable.

Transition

If the opening doesn't flow easily into the thesis statement, you will have to add words to link the two. The additional words are called a transition. Sometimes only a phrase is needed, sometimes just one sentence, and at other times you'll need more explanation to smoothly link the opening to the thesis.

Thesis Statement

After you choose and write one of the four openings – quote, question, comment, or story – and add a transition if needed, type the thesis statement exactly as you have it at the top of the outline.

Elements of Your Outline

The next sentence following your thesis statement should begin, "This paper will discuss…" Then list the main sections of your outline. Depending upon the approach, the word "discuss" can be replaced by another word that will make the sentence more accurate to your particular paper. Examples of alternate word choices include: prove, show, examine, evaluate, propose, or expose.

Let's pull the introduction together. Look back at the example outline on page 26 and let's use it as our example. Let's pretend we are writing an introduction for the paper that is outlined there. The elements to be included in the introduction may look like this:

Opening: Quote –	"A freeloader is a confirmed guest. He is the man who is always willing to come to dinner." Damon Runyon, *Short Takes*, "Freeloading Ethics."
Transition:	A freeloader is a person who does not work but mooches off of others. The government-assistance program in the United States has created an entire social class of freeloaders.
Thesis Statement:	I believe the welfare system is so problematic that it should be abolished.
Elements of the	The paper will discuss the background of the welfare system, exposes its
Outline:	problems, proves how these problems negatively affect society, and poses the solutions by suggesting alternatives to the problems.

Combined as one smooth block then, this introduction would read as follows:

> In the book *Short Takes*, Damon Runyon says, "A freeloader is a confirmed guest. He is the man who is always willing to come to dinner. Yes, a freeloader is a person who does not work but mooches off others. The government-assistance program in the United States has created an entire social class of freeloaders. I believe the welfare system is so problematic that it should be abolished. The paper will discuss the background of the welfare system, expose its problems, prove how these problems negatively affect society, and pose the solutions by suggesting alternatives to the problems.

Now, use the Term Paper Introduction Template provided on the next page to plan the introduction to your term paper. When you complete the template, combine the elements (which may take more than one paragraph) into a smooth block.

Term Paper Introduction Template

Open with:

    A. Quote about _____

_____

_____

    B. Question about _____

_____

_____

    C. Comment about _____

_____

_____

    D. Story about _____

_____

_____

_____

_____

_____

_____

_____

Transition: _____

_____

_____

Thesis Statement: _____

_____

_____

_____

Elements of your outline: This paper will discuss _____

_____

_____

_____

_____

9

WRITE YOUR PRELIMINARY CONCLUSION

Why write the conclusion before you're even finished with the sections? This is done because you want to keep the destination always in mind. This step will keep you on track. Writing your paper is like going on a trip with the conclusion as the ultimate destination. Every section must lead toward that destination or that section is not necessary for the journey. By writing a preliminary conclusion now, you are able to keep it in mind. As you write each section, ask yourself, "Does this section help lead my readers to my conclusion?"

For example, if your paper is about keeping marijuana illegal, you would write out your convictions. Then, as you write the sections of your paper, continually compare each section to the preliminary conclusion to be sure that the section does not contradict the conclusion.

10

WRITE THE SECTIONS AND INCLUDE YOUR ENDNOTES

Let's get your sections going. Print out a copy of your finalized outline and set it up to one side of your computer. Keep a pen handy to check off each section as you complete drafting it. Read what the outline says next to Roman numeral two (II). Now pull out all the notes you've written from the research related to this section. Read through those notes and put them in order. Decide what you will talk about first, what next, etc. Once all your notes are in order, place them to the other side of the computer.

You can now draft in one of two ways. Combine your notes by using pen and paper and write out the section before typing. Each chapter of this book I wrote on a yellow legal pad, editing along the way. Then on my computer I copied my final draft. It took a while to stop drafting this way because it felt comfortable letting my words flow from my brain through my hand and out onto the paper. Of course I've been writing before personal computers even existed. Let's not go there.

The second draft option is to put your ideas together by typing straight from your notes. If you choose to draft this way, keep the screen single-spaced to see more of what you're writing. Also realize that this is only the first draft. If you type straight from your notes, you will have the tendency to believe there's no need to check it over. That section is not done simply because it's typed. Force yourself to read it over when you finish typing out the section. Look for mistakes and listen for how your ideas flow.

Whichever way you decide to draft, the most important thing to remember is: WRITE THE INFORMATION IN YOUR OWN WORDS. Close the books, put the articles away, and turn off the television. Use your notes only as a guide. You do not have a doctorate degree and are not the expert, the paper should only sound like you not any other author.

Plagiarism is a serious infraction. You can be kicked out of college and lose scholarships if caught. You will be guilty of plagiarism if the words of the author are copied and presented as your own. You are supposed to be reporting about what you have learned. Do this by using your own words.

Don't try the middle school trick either of taking the author's sentences and changing a few words with the use of a thesaurus. This is plagiarism too. That author's sentence was his or her idea, not yours. To avoid plagiarism, go through our outline one point at a time. Read everything you have gathered about that point. Then put all those books, articles, and notes aside and write out what you have to say about that point.

Endnotes

From time to time throughout your paper, you will need to prove that all comments are accurate. Let readers know where your facts and statistics have come from. To do this, include the information in a list known as the endnotes. Endnotes are the same as footnotes, except endnotes are typed in a list located at the end of your paper and footnotes are listed at the bottom of the page where the reference is made. DO NOT USE BOTH! Ask your professor which he/she wants. For purposes of this book, we will use endnotes.

When it's time to use an endnote, place a little number – a superscript - behind the sentence. If using Microsoft Word (version earlier than 2007), this is found under "Insert" on the toolbar. On the menu, move the cursor down to "Reference." Beside "Reference," click "Footnote." Another menu will appear. On the new menu, click "Endnote." When the computer shows the endnote screen, indent the first line, type in the name of the author, the source, and the page number if applicable that refers to whatever you are referencing. Then click "Close" to get back to the original document. The computer will have placed the superscript (the little number) at the spot where you stopped to type the endnote.

After you have typed the endnote and clicked "Close," the endnote will seem to disappear. Don't panic. It's still there, only it's at the end of your document. If you want to see it, go to the "File" menu, click "Print Preview," and you will see where your endnote went.

You may want to use quotes as proof for the points made in your paper. That's okay as long as the quote is proof of what you are reporting and not the point itself. Quotes must be accurate, enclosed in quotations marks, and relatively short. Use them strategically only when necessary to strengthen your point, not to pad your page count. Overuse of quotes could result in a lower grade. The instructor will see through your attempt at having enough pages by sticking in lots of quotes. How will your instructor know? Other than the fact that this is an old trick that she probably tried to use herself, she will notice that your paper has long or lots of quotes and little substance. Still, when using quotes, be sure to endnote them.

I once had a student who wrote his whole paper as quotes. He figured that as long as he included an endnote for each one, he would not be guilty of plagiarism and all his facts would be straight. Nice try, but no cigar. Again, the term paper has to be written in your own words, show what you've learned and wish to report about your topic. Quotes, facts, and statistics simply back up what you are trying to say.

Now is also the time to ask the instructor if your paper should be typed in MLA (Modern Language Association) or APA (American Psychological Association) format. Information will not change, but the way you type the endnotes, bibliography, and other little things, will. Below are examples of the differences between MLA and APA format styles:

MLA Bibliography (Works Cited) Entry	APA Bibliography (Works Cited) Entry
Elliott, Sharon Norris. The Stupid Term Paper. South Gate: OceanRose Publishing, 2003	Elliott, S.N. (2003). The Stupid Term Paper. South Gate: OceanRose Publishing.
MLA Endnote Entry	APA Parenthetical Citation
[5]Sharon Norris Elliott, The Stupid Term Paper (South Gate: OceanRose Publishing, 2002) 51-52.	Do not use endnotes or footnotes. Right within the text, immediately following the fact or quote, just put the author's last name, a comma, and the publication year of the work from which you are quoting. (Elliott, 2003)

Add P.E.P.

So again, write through everything you have beside and under Roman numeral two (II) from your outline. Then move on to everything beside and under Roman numeral three (III), and so on until the paper is finished. To flesh out each section, add P.E.P.

The first "P" stands for "point." State your point clearly. Use a strong, well-worded topic sentence and follow that up with other sentences, written in varying sentence patterns, which make your point clear.

The "E" stands for "examples." Explain your point by giving readers an example of what you're talking about. Find these examples as you read through your sources and interview people in regard to your paper.

The second "P" stands for "proof." Follow up your point with some kind of proof – a fact, a statistic, or a quote – to show that the point is valid. Insert an endnote to let the reader know from where your examples, facts, statistics, and quotes came.

To make your term paper interesting, don't use these letters in this order every time. For some sections, start with the example and let that lead to the point. In other sections, you might state a startling statistic first.

Okay, get to work!

11

COMPOSE YOUR FINAL CONCLUSION

All sections should now be drafted, typed in, and edited. You do realize that editing is part of the writing process, don't you? Now read over your preliminary conclusion. Revise to be sure that all of your points have clearly led to the planned conclusion.

Your term paper is almost completed but not quite yet. Someone once said that anyone can stop writing, but only a writer can finish. A conclusion has been reached. So what? You need some way to wrap up, to bring the paper in for a smooth landing. Just as the introduction got you started and accelerated the term paper up the on-ramp and onto the highway, the conclusion slows you down, decelerates you down the off-ramp, and brings your paper to a gentle end.

Here are five ways to achieve this smooth finish.

Connect to your Introduction

First, find a way to connect the conclusion to the introduction. Perhaps you chose to start with a story lead. Work the end of the same story into your conclusion. Of course, the end of the story must make the case for, agree with, or prove the conclusion the term paper has reached.

For example, if you began your paper about the problems of the welfare system with the story of a family who has been stuck in that system for three generations, you could end that paper telling how 15-year-old Ishauna is now pregnant and applying for welfare, making this the fourth generation in the system.

Tell Your Audience What to Do

The second way you can end is by telling the audience what you want them to do about the conclusion the paper has reached. If your paper concerns some controversial topic such as cloning, abortion, or homosexual marriage, you may want your reader to change his/her former viewpoint. The paper may concern a topic that affects society. You may want your reader to contact a Congressman to try to get legislation passed on the issue you discussed. Agreement with your conclusion might require the reader to change his/her behavior. Depending on your conclusion, end the paper by suggesting a course of action for the reader to take.

Reveal Your Personal Changes

Third, your term paper may hit a very personal nerve. An interesting ending would be an explanation of how the conclusion directly affects or affected you and what you did or plan to do about it. For example, if your paper is about the dangers of teenage obesity and you were an obese teen, your paper could end by explaining some of the health benefits now enjoyed because you lost weight.

Show the Logical Outcome

Fourth, the conclusion can detail the logical outcome of the issue you've discussed. If the paper suggests that cloning is great for society, your conclusion could give the reader a picture of what the family structure could be like if cloning was an everyday occurrence.

Combine Several Types of Endings

Finally, the conclusion could be a combination of some of the above ideas. For instance, you might discuss the logical outcome of agreeing with your issue and then suggest that the reader support legislation in favor of that issue. Or explain the effect the issue has had personally and use that as strong proof of why the reader should change his/her viewpoint.

Use the conclusion template on the following page to plan, and then draft your conclusion.

Conclusion Template

Transition from final section to conclusion: _____

_____

_____

_____

_____

(Now choose one, or a logical combination of several, of the following methods to outline your conclusion.)

Connect to Your Introduction:_____

_____

_____

_____

_____

Tell Your Audience What to Do:_____

_____

_____

_____

_____

Reveal Your Personal Changes:_____

_____

_____

_____

_____

Show the Logical Outcome: _____

_____

_____

_____

_____

Combine Several Types of Endings: _____

_____

_____

_____

_____

12

FORMAT YOUR BIBLIOGRAPHY
(WORKS CITED)

Congratulations, part one! You've finished writing all parts of the text – the introduction, the body, and the conclusion. I'll give you the other half of your congratulations at the very end. Hang in there. Believe it or not, you are almost done.

It's now time to format your bibliography. As you should already know, the bibliography is the list that shows all the books used while researching your topic. Even if only a book or magazine article was used for background research, still list it in the bibliography.

There are several things to remember to correctly write the bibliography:

1. At the top of the page, entitle your list "Works Cited." Why not call it a bibliography? Perhaps it's because it is clear that you haven't actually read all the books. Frankly, I really don't know. I just know that the correct title to use is "Works Cited" and this title belongs centered at the top of the first page of your bibliography.

2. The point of the bibliography is to allow readers the opportunity to go to the same sources you used to do some additional reading on their own. With this

in mind, you can understand why it's important to include all the identifying information. This would include the following:

- ✓ Author's name
- ✓ Title of the work (the book, magazine, website, etc.)
- ✓ Title of the article (if within a magazine, journal, etc.)
- ✓ Publisher
- ✓ Publisher's city and publication date

The nature of the source will dictate the information included in your bibliography. There are lots of sources readily available that will show you how to write bibliography entries.

3. While compiling your bibliography, double-check to be sure you've used at least three different types of sources.
4. Be sure that every reference used as an endnote is also listed in your bibliography.
5. Check to be sure the bibliography is typed in the correct format – MLA or APA.
6. Once your list is completely compiled, alphabetize it according to the first letter in each entry.
7. Your bibliography (works cited) should begin on the page following the endnotes. So, if your term paper takes up the minimum of 15 full pages, one page of endnotes will be page 16, and the bibliography will begin on page 17. If your paper is 19 pages long, two pages of endnotes will be pages 20-21, and your bibliography will begin on page 22.

All right, type out your bibliography.

13

THE FINAL CHECK

#1   Print out the final copy of your outline:
- ✓ Top center, entitle this "Outline." Use capital letters and lower case letters, no quotation marks, and no underlining.
- ✓ Begin the page with your thesis statement.
- ✓ Be sure your outline uses properly indented Roman numerals, capital letters, numbers, and lower case letters.
- ✓ In MLA format, include your last name and page numbers in lower case Roman numerals, in the upper right corner.

#2   Remember:
- ✓ At 12-point size, Times New Roman font, there will be 22-23 lines per page, double-spaced. This means if you type a 15-page paper, you should have at least 330 typed lines. Any less than this means your paper is short and points will be deducted.
- ✓ If you want to include pictures, and place them within the text, your page count will have to compensate for the number of lines the picture took up. So, if the picture takes up 5 lines on page 7 of your paper,

you will have to type at least 5 lines of text on page 16 to have a full paper. The best way to add pictures is to refer to them parenthetically within the text and then place them on numbered pages at the end of the paper before the endnotes and bibliography.

✓ The 15-20 page limit does not include the endnotes and bibliography. You must type 15-20 pages of quality text. (See pages 1, 27, and 50).

✓ Use at least three (3) different types of sources. (See chapter 7)

#3   Before printing out the final copy of text look at the pages on your computer screen. Be sure:

✓ There are no extra spaces between lines and paragraphs.

✓ Your lines are double-spaced.

✓ The sections are not separated with headers. Transitions from one section to another are simply made by the wording you use in the new paragraph.

✓ You have used 12-point, Times New Roman font only.

✓ You have at least 15 full pages, but not more than 20 full pages, of text.

✓ Your endnotes are on their own page(s).

✓ Your bibliography (works cited) begins on its own page.

✓ The pages are consecutively numbered and each page has the proper header. For MLA format, that means your last name and page number goes in the upper right corner of each page,

✓ You have proofread, spell-checked, and deleted repetitious sections.

#4   In a new file type your cover sheet then print it out.

MLA Format

```
┌─────────────────────────┐
│                         │
│          Title          │
│                         │
│                         │
│          Byline         │
│                         │
│                         │
│          Date           │
│        Professor        │
│                         │
└─────────────────────────┘
```

#5   Print out the entire paper

- Use regular, 20 lb., 8 ½ X 11 white typing papers.
- Use black ink only.
- Arrange the complete paper in this order:
  * Cover Sheet
  * Outline
  * Text
  * Pictures (if any)
  * Endnotes
  * Works Cited (bibliography)
- Do not put the paper in any special binding unless instructed to do so by your professor. Simply use one heavy-duty staple in the upper left corner.
- Print out, and make a second copy. Your instructor may require two copies or the second copy can be insurance against possible loss or destruction of the first copy. (i.e. the puppy wet on it, your little sister thought it was a coloring book, your dad used it as a coaster, etc.)

Now, congratulations, part two! You are totally finished. Go turn in your masterpiece and treat yourself to a movie. You deserve it!

Sample Term Paper

The Color Green
Le Vert de Couleur

By Jehoshua Brown

English IV
Mrs. Elliott
January 7, 2009

The Color Green
Le Vert de Couleur
Outline

Thesis Statement: Going green is worth it if we plan to preserve life on our planet.

I. Introduction

II. List different things wrong with the environment

    A. Acid Rain

    B. Global Warming

        1. Greenhouse Gases

    C. Air Pollution

    D. Hazardous Waste

    E. Ozone Depletion

    F. Rain forest destruction

    G. Green Technology/Energy

III. Tell exactly how humans contributed to each environmental problem

    A. Acid Rain

    B. Global Warming

        1. Greenhouse Gases

    C. Air Pollution

    D. Hazardous Waste

        1. Not recycling

        2. Unsafe products

E. Ozone Depletion

F. Rain forest destruction

G. Green Technology/Energy

IV. Tell what can or will happen if nothing is done.

    A. Unhealthy air for future generations

    B. Unsanitary foods or droughts and no food

    C. Unnatural Disasters

V. State what is being done to fix the environment and how everyone can help.

    A. Acid Rain

    B. Global Warming

        1. Greenhouse Gases

        2. Lifestyle changes to help save energy and help cut down on greenhouse gases

    C. Air Pollution

        1. The Tree Way

    D. Hazardous Waste

        1. Not recycling

        2. Unsafe products

    E. Ozone Depletion

    F. Rain forest destruction

        1. The Tree Way

Le Vert de Couleur
The Color Green

"I can't breathe!" you scream as you wake up one Wednesday morning in the near future. Your room is dark and the air is thick and dry. You jump from your bed and run into the living room to find someone. No one is there. You check all the rooms. Still no one. The whole house is dark. There are no lights on or any curtains open. Still struggling to breathe easily, you open the windows to let some air in. When you open the window you see that all of the green life is gone and the air looks murky. You do not see any of your neighbors out, you don't hear any birds singing, and you can't see the sky clearly. To get a better look, you step outside and face extreme heat. It feels like you're in an oven. Through the dark foggy air, you catch a glimpse of some remnants of the blue sky you've grown to love, but the sky is barely visible and somehow you know that soon you will never see it again. The grass you're standing on is rough, dry and dead. You realize that no amount of water will ever bring it back.

This scenario will not seem so distant if we continue to do nothing about global warming. This term paper elucidates exactly went wrong in the past with the environment, lists things that are wrong with the environment, tells what can or will happen if nothing is done, and explains what is being done to fix the environment issue.

The largest problems in the environment today are acid rain, global warming, air pollution, hazardous waste, and rain forest destruction.[i] These things listed need to be abolished in order to make our world a healthy place.

As defined by Wikipedia.com, acid rain is rain or any other form of precipitation that is unusually acidic. Acid rain mostly affects plants, which give off oxygen, and water animals which we eat. It is caused by the release of sulfur and nitrogen. The sulfur and nitrogen form a compound when met that reacts with the atmosphere which creates acid.[ii] Acid rain also affects human health. Scientists have shown that acid rain can cause illness and even death. Acid rain can even cause cancer. Why not end acid rain and cancer all at once? If you help fix the environment you also help illness.

Another terrible condition affecting the world is global warming. Some say that it is natural for the Earth to go through cycles of hot and cold. I believe that is what the seasons are for and here is why. Global warming is when the Earth's average temperature of air and oceans are increased. Why the temperature is rising is still being studied, but one of the reasons is the greenhouse effect.[iii]

In 1824 Joseph Fourier discovered the greenhouse effect. He studied "the process by which absorption and emission of infrared radiation by atmospheric gases warm a planet's lower atmosphere and surface." A frequently asked question about the greenhouse effect is. "How does the strength of the greenhouse effect change when human activity increases the atmospheric concentrations of some greenhouse gases?" Since industrial industry increased and expanded, the concentration of the different greenhouse gases has increased as well. Another frequently asked question is. "What are the greenhouse gases and how much damage do they contribute?" Well, major greenhouse gases are water vapor, ozone, methane, and carbon dioxide. Water vapor contributes to 36-76 percent of the GHE (greenhouse effect). Ozone contributes 3-7 percent. Methane contributes 4-9 percent. And carbon dioxide contributes 9-26 percent.[iv]The concentration of carbon dioxide and methane has risen by 31 percent and 149 percent since the mid-1700s. Researchers suspect that the carbon dioxide percentage will rise due to burning fossil fuels, and land use. Of course, the rate also depends on the future of economic, technological and natural developments[v].

Air pollution is another major contributor to the corruption of the Earth's environment. Humans are the reason for air pollution. Humans release smoke into the atmosphere, they drive cars that emit chemicals into the air, and they introduce other chemicals into the air that are harmful to living things. These chemicals do damage to the natural environment. Acid rain and air pollution can be dire. Air pollution is known to cause respiratory disease (disease of the lungs) and even death. A gas that contributes to global warming is also linked to air pollution, and that is carbon dioxide. Although carbon dioxide is needed to help plants regenerate as they go through photosynthesis, it is a major pollutant to the air we breathe. It helps and it hurts.

Hazardous waste is very simple and quite easy to deal with. Frankly, hazardous waste is a type of waste that threatens human or environmental life. In order to be considered hazardous waste, the waste must fall under at least one of these five categories: flammable, oxidizing, corrosive, toxic, or radioactive. Usually hazardous waste is solid and can often be found in our own homes. These wastes are items like paint, batteries, and aerosol cans. Though hazardous waste is a major contribution to destroying the world, there are easy ways to get rid of it. Recycling is a major way to get rid of hazardous waste. If everyone recycled there would be less hazardous waste to affect the public and the environment.

Other ways to get rid of hazardous waste include, neutralizing, landfills (isolation), and waste-to-energy (destruction). Most hazardous waste can all be recycled into new products. If the hazardous product is neutralized it can be processed so that whatever was making the hazardous material hazardous would be eliminated. Neutralizing takes hazardous waste and makes it non-hazardous waste.

Our natural rainforests are depleting. Nowadays, forests have been used for lumber and agriculture clearance. The natural percentage of rainforest that covers the world is shrinking. In Brazil, for example, deforestation has reached dangerous levels. Over the past year, deforestation has risen to nearly 67 percent. By 2030, deforestation will wipe out of damage the Amazon rain forest by 60 percent[vi].

Not only are we losing trees but a lot of animals are on their way to becoming extinct. Edward O. Wilson from Harvard University believes that about 50,000 animals per year are becoming endangered, and if this continues a quarter more of all species on earth could be eradicated over the next 50 years just because humans are taking over their natural habitat. That is a lot of animals that my children and other people in general will never be able to see.

Throughout our daily lives we consume massive amounts of energy. We use energy for heat, food (cooking), transportation, manufacturing (making stuff) etc. We use energy from all those things just to live comfortably, but energy has to come from somewhere right? Yes, the energy we use comes from fossil fuels. Fossil fuels are fossil source fuels like carbon and hydrocarbons that come from the crust of the Earth. They are non-renewable and take millions of years to form. What we have is reducing faster than new ones can grow. Eighty-six percent of energy in the world came from burning fossil fuels in 2005. Fossil fuels are important because when they are burned, they create a large amount of energy. Energy we use is being pulled from a source that is irreplaceable if ever used up.

The use of these fossil fuels can have a bad impact on the environment and the collection of the fossil fuels can be damaging. Collecting fossil fuels can cause oil spills and strip mining. So, if we use fossil fuels for energy and collecting fossil fuels can cause major disasters, shouldn't we learn not to waste the energy that we have, especially when it is such a risk using and retrieving them? Yes we should, wasting energy can eventually lead to catastrophic damages to the environment and catastrophe is the last thing we want to live in.

Acid rain, global warming, air pollution, hazardous waste, ozone depletion, rain forest destruction, and energy waste are all really bad things affecting the world, but how exactly do humans contribute to it?

Acid rain comes from sulfur in the atmosphere. This sulfur comes from coal combustion, smelting of metal, ocean spray, and organic decay. Ninety percent of sulfur in the atmosphere comes from human activity.

Main ways that humans have contributed to global warming is land clearing and burning fossil fuels. The burning of these fossil fuels is usually in electric power plants that give off the energy for office buildings and house utensils, cars, and factories. That's pretty much wherever a person is. Remember, a major cause of global warming is high carbon dioxide percentages. Burning fossil fuels creates carbon dioxide which slows the escape of heat into space. That means that heat stays here and makes it hotter, ergo global warming. Plants absorb carbon from the air and use it for photosynthesis. When land is being cleared, carbon build up is caused because it is not being absorbed from the air.

Air pollution happens by natural causes and human enforcement, but human activity has had a bigger impact on it. Again, the burning of fossil fuels has a large impact to air pollution. Cars that give off fuels are another way we give to air pollution daily. Burning fossil fuels and automobiles that combust fuels together makes 90 percent of the air pollution in the United States.

Many household products have ingredients that when they are thrown away they can cause mischief to some natural resources. Things like motor oil, liquid cleaners, and toilet bowl cleaners have hazardous chemicals and aren't discarded properly. Almost all households contribute to hazardous waste. Uses of things that may be in every house like nail polish, nail polish remover, shoe polish, hairspray, and even some medicines can be hazardous when thrown away. These things are considered hazardous when they are flammable, react differently when introduced to other substances, or are toxic or acidic. These types of things need to be recycled properly to not become a dangerous material to the environment.

Most people never really paid attention to the environment and its issues. Now that the earth is going down a slippery slope most people want to be on board to help recover what we lost. Then and now, people did not recycle much. Recycling conserves energy and the earth's natural resources. If people continue not to recycle, our timber intake would increase by 80 percent to meet our fiber demand. If you recycle, you save more energy than a waste-to-energy factory can produce.

Recycling is a major way to cut down on greenhouse gas release. If people recycle, they are already making an enormous contribution to making the environment healthier. Carbon can be reduced by 10 million metric tons (is equal to 10,000,000,000 kilograms) if the paper and container recycling rate is raised by 10 percent. Not only is that super awesome, but if more people recycle landfill space will be saved. It is also three times cheaper to recycle rather than to use landfills. With every ton of paper recycled about seventeen trees are saved, 79 gallons of oil is preserved, and 7,000 gallons of water is kept. Recycling is a beautiful way of contributing to the conservation of the environment although most people do not do it. "The United States has finally reached a landmark in its paper recycling efforts in 2006 with 53.4% of the paper consumed being recovered for recycling."[vii]

My teacher told me of a television report about the problem of Starbucks and other coffee cups. These types of coffees are very popular, but the cups, and especially the plastic lids, are filling up the landfills. The plastic lids are not recyclable and sometimes the cups aren't either if they are lined with a thin coat of plastic to help them keep the drinks hot. The report suggested that we buy the reusable, silver type of thermos coffee cups. Take them in and have them filled with the coffee you want to drink each morning. This will drastically reduce the waste caused by the paper cups.

Most people like to eat beef, right? For every quarter-pound hamburger made from rainforest beef, 55 square feet of rainforest is destroyed. That's the size of a living room. Six hundred and sixty pounds of rainforest life is killed to produce one pound of food. Rainforests are used to raise cattle. Why? Because it's cheaper. Poor countries like the ones listed above in section one are willing to sell rainforest land for funds. The beef-raising companies move in and sweep clear the amount of land needed. They burn the forests and use the ashes as nutrients for the cows and beef animals to eat. After about a season or two the natural nutrients fade away and the company moves on to another piece of land. After a couple of years of using the rain forest as grazing grounds, the land becomes so terrible it cannot even be used as that. It becomes a dry patch and could never return back.

Once the forests are completely gone, rains come and floods do even more damage. Rain forest destruction isn't just bad for animals and nutrients. When rain forests are burnt down, tons of carbon dioxide is released into the air, which is a major in factor in global warming. Thus, one section of a rain forest burned affects the whole world. There is part of a rainforest burning all the time. During the 1960's 25 percent of the Central American rain forests were burned for beef production that was imported to Europe and the U.S. Also, in Brazil 38 percent of rain forests were burned for beef production. When our rain forests are being burned and depleted, think about the happy California cow, or that burger you are eating. When you eat a hamburger there is a large chance that that meat came from a cattle ranch that used to be a forest. You can very well be an accomplice to the destruction of our rain forests and global warming. Ooh, isn't that dreadful.

If the people in the world continue to disregard the global warming issues and fossil fuel issue, in future generations we can have terrible air quality. The carbon dioxide percentage will continue to rise and will continue to stop the heat from escaping into space. If this happens, the ozone will continue to deteriorate and it will be forever hot on Earth. As we know, it will take a large amount of time and large amounts of work to try and reshape the environment to become as it used to be. But if we do not do anything, the chance of the environment ever becoming leveled and correct again will be much higher and much harder to achieve. Not only will global warming take such a toll on the earth in generations to come, but the air pollution percentage will rise and create unhealthy air to breathe. With rain forest destruction, trees will not be around to absorb the carbon and discharge clean oxygen.

The future is not doomed to forever be in bad environmental shape. There are things being done to reduce the iniquities that are affecting our environment now. Acid rain, global warming, air pollution, hazardous waste, ozone depletion, rain forest destruction, and energy waste, are not permanent troubles to our world; they can all be fixed with your help, of course.

Most of all, electricity we use comes from burning fossil fuels. When acid decomposes from the burning of fossil fuels, sulfur and nitrogen oxides are released... Coal is a very important fossil fuel in the U.S but it also takes credit for emitting most of the sulfur and nitrogen oxide into the atmosphere. The sulfur in coal is not pure, so it reacts with the air when negatively when coal is burned for its energy. Air pollution causes acid rain. Basically, cleaning the air and reducing air pollution reduces acid rain. Instead of using fossil fuels as a main energy source, we can get energy from other sources; solar energy, wind energy, etc. The chemicals that are given off by the fossil fuels when they are burned pollute the air and causes acid rain. If burning the fossil fuels does something negative to the environment the smartest thing to do is to stop burning and use another energy source.

So what can individuals do to clean up this mess? I'm glad you asked.

If you drive a lot or know someone who is always spending up gas in their vehicle, tell them to slow themselves. Everyone knows that gas from cars pollutes the air. Another good way to help is to plant a tree. Trees absorb the bad air and put out good cleaner air. Most people now plant trees in parks. One tree can make a world of difference, and they make places look pretty and provide shade. Plant shrubbery around your house, not only is it good for the air but in the winter months the plants absorb heat and keeps your home warm and in the summer does the opposite effect. They save energy instead of using gas or electricity to cool or warm your home. Saving energy is a great thing to do to help reduce acid rain. If burning fossil fuels for energy is negative for the environment, saving energy so that less fossil fuel can be burned is a great contribution. Cut off all electronics that are not being used. Lights, televisions, fans, radios, anything that is not being used needs to be off to conserve energy.

If you do one thing to help preserve the environment, you are usually killing two birds with one stone. Things that you do to reduce the effect of global warming could also help air pollution or energy conservation. One thing like recycling can solve a number of environmental issues.

Global warming is one of the major issues involving the world that we are faced with today. Of course, like mentioned before, it is not a permanent problem. Something that I do that you can also do to contribute to the fight against global warming is the most simple: recycling. Paper, plastic, newspaper, glass and aluminum cans, anything that can be recycled is worth recycling because if you just cut your household waste in half, you can save near 2,400 pounds of carbon dioxide. That is a lot of deadly chemical that is not affecting us.

Use less air conditioning and heat. There are other ways to get the heat and air conditioning that you need without wasting so much energy, and it saves you money.

Get vents (insulation) to your walls or in your attic and install weather stripping around all of your doors and windows. This reduces the amount of energy you need to heat your home and saves you at least 25 percent on your bill. Instead of having the heat on full blast all the time, cut it down when you are sleeping or when you are away. No one is there to enjoy the warmth, but when you get home your house will be warm and toasty. When you lower your thermostat in the winter and higher in the summer by two degrees, you save at least 2,000 pounds of carbon.

Recycling and cutting your thermostat up or down depending on the season saves 4,400 pounds of carbon each year. Imagine if more people did that. Another thing that I do, that saves energy and money is switching light bulbs. They are brighter, last longer, and cheaper. Replace all of your regular light bulbs with CFL (compact florescent light) bulbs. When you replace on 60 watt bulb will save over 30 dollars over the life of that bulb. A CFL bulb last 10 times longer than a normal bulb, uses two-thirds less energy and gives off 70 percent less heat. If every United States household replaced their light bulbs with CFL bulbs, which is the equivalent of taking 7.5 million cars off the road by eliminating 90 billion pounds of greenhouse gases. If you have outdoor lighting, make sure that the lights are off during the day. Outdoor lighting is a major waste when homeowners forget to cut off the lights during the day. If you own outdoor lights, buy the lights that have detectors that only come on after dark or when they detect motion or heat. Solar-powered lights convert the sunlight into electricity therefore never wasting energy.

Emissions are a major cause of global warming, and a major cause of emissions is driving. Besides saving money and gasoline walking places or skating or using any type of non-motor vehicle is usually good exercise. You lose pounds and you save money and the world, how great is that? Make sure that when driving that the car is functioning properly. Make sure that the tires are properly inflated because that can improve your gas mileage about a good three percent. Every gallon of gas you save not only saves gas and money, but keeps 20 pounds of carbon out of the air. Buy a new car, and other energy efficient products. Buy a car with good gas mileage. The safest thing to do when buying an energy efficient car is buying hybrid. Hybrids are more fuel efficient than normal cars. Choose home appliances that are also energy efficient. Try not to buy things that are over-packaged, like things with molded plastic and all packaging that cannot be recycled. Trimming down on your household waste by as little as ten percent, will save 1,200 pounds of carbon dioxide annually.

Hot and cold water makes a difference in global warming. It's all about saving energy and saving carbon from getting into the atmosphere. Buy a low-flow shower head to save water and 350 pounds of carbon a year. Setting your water heater to 120 degrees saves plenty of energy and keeps your water warm. Instead of using hot water, use warm or cold water to wash your clothes. Hot water requires energy to make it hot. Using warm or cold, uses less energy. Just using warm or cold water can save 500 pounds of carbon in most homes yearly. Electricity is another place where most people go wrong and waste major amounts of energy. Do not be that person. If it isn't in use, or isn't need switch it off.

Plant a tree. During the photosynthesis process, plants absorb carbon and give off oxygen. There are too few of trees to offset the damage of carbon that is being put off daily by humans. One tree will absorb one ton of carbon in its entire lifetime. Plant a tree, save a generation. The Urban Tree Foundation is an agency that provides services to benefit California's forest. Their main focus is to plant and conserve tree life in California since 1999. They have an assortment of trees that can be planted based on where the tree is needed to be planted. They teach about why conserving forest and planting trees are important and collaborate with other private and public agencies to make the communities a cleaner and greater place. Support agencies like UTF and make a drastic difference in yours and other people's lives.

Most utility companies give free energy audits to help people see where they are not using energy wisely in their home. It is good if you take advantage of that service. Some may even offer some type of rebate program to pay for the energy efficient upgrades after the inspection. But most importantly, a great and one of the most effective way to help stop global warming is tell other people about everything you know about the situation. Informing others about recycling and energy conservation will obviously spread the word, but it will make a difference because it is one more person, one more family saving 500 hundred pounds of carbon per year and so forth. With less energy means that we do not need the fossil fuels that create greenhouse gases as much and global warming will have less of an impact on our lives.

In most homes, family comes first. In order to keep our homes clean and healthy we use things that are not exactly safe for the environment and when we are finished with them, we do not dispose of them properly. Hazardous waste is 100 percent preventable.

Make sure that all aerosol cans that are used are completely empty before throwing them away. Spray all of the contents in the can into a cardboard box, or onto a cardboard surface. Let the cardboard dry and throw it away along with the empty can. This way less of the chemicals escape into the atmosphere and the once hazardous waste is now just waste. Not all hazardous products can just be tossed away empty.

When you buy something, read the label because it tells you how to use it and dispose of it properly. Avoid all products that have any type of "caution," or "dangerous," signs on the label because those tend to be bad for the environment. When dealing with bad materials, it is good to get the right amount of whatever it is that you need. Over-stocking will raise your homes' hazardous waste material, cost more money, and put you in more of a risk of poisoning.

A smart and cautious thing to do in order to stay healthy is to never mix chemicals. For example, let's say you are running low on Lysol and Mr. Clean, so you pour them together to make one full bottle of super cleaner. That can end dreadfully. That mixture can be toxic or produce a harmful gas. Use on product entirely, the way you're supposed to use it, and then make sure it is empty. This way, you are safe from any hazardous material and you help reduce the percentage of hazardous material in the U.S.

My aunt buys environmentally friendly cleaning supplies. Her favorite to use is Green Works cleaners. Green works is a product of Clorox. There are no harsh chemicals found in green works that can harm you or the environment.

No one likes to waste energy. Wasting energy will eventually take a toll on our natural resource. To reduce the chances of running out of natural resources we should try to use the energy we have now wisely.

Home appliances are major sources of energy lose. Cut your refrigerator down; they use about 20 percent of home electricity. Also, make sure that the energy saver switch on your refrigerator is on. Make sure that your dishwasher is full when use it and cut off the automatic drying. Allow your dishes to air dry if you can, not using the heat can save 20 percent of energy that your dishwasher uses. Unplug all of your appliances whenever you can when they are not in use. United States consumers spend 5 billion dollars annually just on standby power, which is about 5 percent of all the electricity in the country.

Again, try to buy energy efficient appliances and update all appliances that are not energy efficient. Newer pieces of equipment have an Energy Star Label and those should be bought. If you have an air conditioner or heating system, replace the air filter. You lose a lot of energy when they air system has to work hard to get air out through a dirty filter. Just cleaning the dirty filter can save you 5 percent of energy it uses, and 175 pounds of carbon a year. Improve your home with updates. Change your windows to argon filled double-glazed windows. With gas heat, these windows save 2.4 tons of carbon yearly. Plant a tree that can cast a shade. If you live in cold climate paint your house a dark color and if in a warm temperature area paint it a light color. Shade trees reduce energy use and the painting of your house a different color may save at least 2.4 pounds or carbon annually. Other helpful hints found in the global warming section also apply for this energy conservation.

"Mirror mirror on the wall, who is the Greenest of them all?"[viii]Everyone wants to look good, but sometimes the latest things to stay looking young and flawless are not exactly eco-friendly. In order for a "natural" skin care product to be called natural, it only needs at least 1 percent natural ingredients. The rest can be processed and manmade. Your skin absorbs 60 percent of anything applied to your skin. Throughout a year, your skin can absorb 4.4 pounds of non-natural chemicals. Stay healthy and keep the environment healthy by looking at all of the ingredients on the label. Buy oils that are made from fruit seeds and nuts. Baby oil and mineral oils is a by-product of gasoline production. Over a hundred million gallons of mineral oil/baby oil is used in the U.S each year, which is equal to 25 percent of the use gas in the United States daily. Use bar sap instead of liquid soap. Bar soap is less expensive and it saves packaging waste. If every home replaced a bottle of body wash with a bar of soap 2.5millions pounds of plastic containers would not be in landfills or other waste streams.

Going green is worth it. Do it for you, for your children and for your environment. It isn't hard to make minor changes in your life to preserve something that you need to survive. The Earth is all we have; we cannot ruin it and go somewhere else when it gets too chaotic. Do what you can today to make your world a better place for you.

You wake up one day in the near future to the sound of birds singing. Your room is filled with natural sunlight and fresh air. Walking into the living room you see family members smiling and feeling happy. On your way to taking the bottles to the recycling can you notice the clear blue sky and the sun shining down on you; a smile sweeps across your face. You inhale a deep breath of clear healthy, carbon free air and you feel good inside. The grass below you is the deepest of green and full of life. The trees in your back yard are blooming apples and the birds above you are singing and flying about. You wave to your neighbors outside who are installing solar powered outdoor lighting on your way into the house. Your day could never get any better and you are filled with joy.

This scenario will not seem so distant if you do something about global warming and the environment.

Endnotes

---

[i] See "Environmental Problems"

[ii] See Wikipedia "Acid Rain"

[iii] See Wikipedia "Global Warming"

[iv] See Wikipedia "Global Warming; Greenhouse effect"

[v] See Wikipedia "Global Warming; Greenhouse effect"

[vi] See Wikipedia "Rain forest destruction"

[vii] See "More Recycling Facts"

Works Cited

"Acid Rain." <u>Wikipedia</u> 23 Nov 2008 25 Nov 2008
<http://en.wikipedia.org/wiki/Acid_Rain>.

Caroline, David, Michael, Mindy, Neil, and Vikas, "Environmental Problems."
<u>ThinkQuest Internet contest</u> 1999 25 Nov 2008
<http://library.thinkquest.org/26026/Environmental_Problems/environmental_proble
ms.html>.

Cooper, James. "Energy Blowing in the Wind." 9 Oct 2008
<http://www.authorizedarticles.com/environment/energy-blowing-in-the-wind.html>.

Corkern, Aydan. "THE MELTING ARCTIC- WHERE IS THE WATER GOING." 9
Oct 2008 <http://www.morethanarticles.com/environment/the-melting-arctic--where-
is-the-water-going.html>.

Dorfman, Josh. <u>The Lazy Environmentalist: Your Guide to Easy, Stylish, Green
Living</u>. New York: Stewart, Tabori & Chang, 2007.

"Household Hazardous Waste." 2. 3 Jan 2009
<http://www.tchd.org/pdfs/household_hazardous_waste.pdf>.

Lowman, Margaret (Meg). "Ecotourism and Its Impact on Forest Conservation." <u>An
ActionBioscience.org original article</u> Aug 2004 1. 6 Oct 2008
<http://www.actionbioscience.org/environment/lowman.html>.

McDilda, Diane Gow. <u>The Everything Green Living Book</u>. Avon, MA: Adams
Media, 2007.

Rogers, Kostigen, Elizabeth, Thomas M. . <u>The Green Book</u>. New York: Three Rivers
Press, 2007.

Scorecard, Power. "20 Things You Can Do to Conserve Energy." <u>Eco-Mall</u> 3 Jan
2009 <http://www.ecomall.com/greenshopping/20things.htm>.

Shah, Anup. "Environmental Issues." <u>Global Issues</u> 14, Feb 2007 1. 6 Oct 2008 <http://www.globalissues.org/issue/168/environmental-issues>.

"The Environmental Effects of Wasting Energy." <u>Energy Conservation</u>30/Jun/2008 3 Jan 2009 <http://www.fluorescentefficiency.com/articles/the-environmental-effects-of-wasting-energy/>.

Tierny, John. "A Gift From the '70s: Energy Lessons ." <u>The New York Times</u> 08 Oct 2008 1. 6 Oct 2008 <http://www.nytimes.com/2008/10/07/science/07tier.html?_r=1&ref=environment&o ref=slogin>.

<u>Too Hot Not to Handle</u>. Dir. Maryann DeLeo and Ellen Goosenberg Kent. DVD. HBO, 2006.

Trask, Crissy. <u>It's Easy Being Green:A Handbook for Earth-Friendly Living</u>. First . Layton, Utah: Gibb Smith, 2006.

"Working together for a Greener Environment." <u>Environment-Green</u> 1. 3 Jan 2009 <http://www.environment-green.com/More_Recycling_Facts_and_Sta tistics.html>.

CBA

8447671R0

Made in the USA
Charleston, SC
10 June 2011